Octave Scales
for the Cello

book one

by Cassia Harvey

CHP115

C. Harvey Publications®   All Rights Reserved.
www.charveypublications.com - print books & free sheet music blog
www.learnstrings.com - downloadable books & chamber music

Octave Scales

Book One

Cassia Harvey

©2005 C. Harvey Publications All Rights Reserved.

Octave Scales for the Cello, Book One

2

©2005 C. Harvey Publications All Rights Reserved.

3

Octave Scales for the Cello, Book One

4

5

Octave Scales for the Cello, Book One

6

©2005 C. Harvey Publications All Rights Reserved.

7

Octave Scales for the Cello, Book One

8

9

Octave Scales for the Cello, Book One

10

11

Octave Scales for the Cello, Book One

12

13

Octave Scales for the Cello, Book One

14

15

16

17

Octave Scales for the Cello, Book One

18

19

Octave Scales for the Cello, Book One

20

©2005 C. Harvey Publications All Rights Reserved.

21

Octave Scales for the Cello, Book One

22

23

Octave Scales for the Cello, Book One

24

25

Octave Scales for the Cello, Book One

26

www.ingramcontent.com/pod-product-compliance
Lightning Source LLC
Chambersburg PA
CBHW051431070526
44584CB00023B/3675